Heaven:
Pushing Up Daisies Ain't So Scary

A Lighthearted Look At A Serious Subject

By Marie Penrose

This book is dedicated to all those who are afraid of death and don't know they don't have to be.

All rights reserved.
This publication cannot be reproduced or transmitted by any means or format without the expressed written permission from
Pen-Rose Editions, Corp.
Reviewers do have permission to quote brief passages of this book for their reviews and testimonials.

Published by
Pen-Rose Editions, Corp
11605 Meridian Market View
Unit 124, Suite 335
Falcon, CO 80831
Contact us at:
E-mail:PenRoseEditions@gmail.com
Web Site:
www.penroseeditionsandpublishing.com

ISBN-13: 978-1942819080
ISBN-10: 1942819080

First Edition 2015
Printed/Published in the United States of America
Heaven: Pushing Up Daisies Ain't So Scary
Copyright 2015 Pen-Rose Editions, Corp

Preface

What a joyful journey compiling this book has been! Strangely enough, what started out as a casual curiosity became almost an obsession to me. It began after an unexpected conversation I had with a dear Christian man at church. It was a sunny Thursday morning and I had arrived early for a weekly Bible study meeting. Seeking some quiet time alone with God in the sanctuary, I sat on the steps at the base of the stage. Unbeknownst to me, the building manager, Steve Brogaard, was also in the sanctuary preparing the room for the upcoming weekend services. After realizing he was there, we began small talk about what was going on in each of our lives. When he found out that I was in the process of searching for answers about heaven and the hereafter, his face went from pleasant to serious and he said he had a story to tell me if I was interested. Disregarding the mental clock in my head, I jumped at the chance to hear his personal testimony.

As we stood in the corner of the sanctuary he proceeded to tell me about his "near death" experience. It had happened over a year earlier when he had asked his wife to take him to the hospital due to an ongoing health issue. He collapsed prior to being admitted though. During the time it took for medical personnel to get to him and finally restart his heart, he said he experienced something unusual and unexpected. He went on to share with me some of the details about what he saw and heard before he was revived. What stood out to me, though, was what he felt in the moments prior to regaining consciousness. He said that, although there weren't human words to adequately describe exactly what he had experienced, the one thing he could say for sure was that he hadn't wanted to come back. He said that where he had gone was so peaceful (and even that word didn't capture how amazing it felt) that he didn't want to return to where he had come from. He went on to tell me how, after being revived the first time, his heart stopped a second time. It was during this second period of being unconscious that he had "seen" his wife, Pam, sitting in a chair in an unfamiliar room completely heart-broken. He said it was that image that caused him to fight back and eventually regain consciousness. After that discussion I couldn't shake that one comment from my mind. "I didn't want to come back." Here was a man who had a wonderful loving wife, many devoted friends and family, and a job he enjoyed yet had been to a place that superseded all that. It was so peaceful and pleasant that he hadn't wanted to return to the life he had known.

That thought fanned the ember of my curiosity into a roaring fire. I bought and devoured a stack of books on the topic of heaven and almost all of them pointed me back to one resource that I already had several versions of…the Bible. So I dug out my huge Strong's Exhaustive Concordance and began to dig even deeper into the topic. My list of research resources grew and included several Bible dictionaries as well as half a dozen Bible commentaries. I relied heavily on several versions of the Bible, most notably the King James Version (KJV), American Standard Version (ASV), and The Bible in Basic English (BBE) which you will see quoted throughout this book. The research and writing seemed to happen simultaneously and I was half way through the first manuscript for this book when I realized that the tone of the book needed to be changed. I had been doing what most of the other authors of the books I had read had done, treated a serious subject seriously. Now don't get me wrong, death is a serious subject and those authors did a great job of illuminating what can be a rather depressing topic. But I kept thinking about what Steve had said and I suddenly felt rather silly. I had become so focused on the death side of heaven that I was missing the heaven side of death. My writing had become too factual instead of hopeful.

So taking the advice of another author to stay true to myself, a person who likes to see the glass as half full rather than half empty, I revised the manuscript by writing it in my own style. I wanted to help those facing their own eminent death or that of a loved one to see that what lies ahead of them is far better than what they will be leaving behind. I wanted to offer hope wrapped up with a little bit of humor. Death doesn't have to be scary, especially if it is looked at as a beginning rather than an ending.

With all of this being said, let me get serious for a moment and state that I have no intention of getting into a lengthy debate about if heaven truly exists. I am also not going to get into a protracted argument in this book about who gets to go there. Those points of contention are for a different place and time by others more willing than myself. The purpose of this book is to try to clarify, as simply as possible, what little is known about this place called "heaven" using the Bible as the main resource and reference, including using some, but definitely not all, verses the Bible contains about the subject of heaven. Then it is up to the reader to decide what they believe or do not believe. I don't claim to know all there is to know about heavenly matters. Far from it. Only God knows the intricate details about the heavenly home most of us are looking forward to. On the contrary, I'm just a fellow seeker trying to find the answers to some of life's basic questions while on this temporary journey to an everlasting home. Come along and join me in the exploration of some of the answers in regards to heaven and the hereafter. Hopefully you will find this quest as interesting as I did.

Table of Contents

Preface	5
Unseen World	9
Looking Back To See Ahead	17
Limitations Of Words	21
No Pain, All Gain (or Retirement In Heaven)	29
Reunions And Rock Stars	39
Eternity Is A Good Thing	47
Traveling Light (or More Heavenly No-No's)	53
Home Sweet Home	57
Let's Get Busy	65
Heaven Inspired Quotes	69

Unseen World

What a daunting task to try to describe or explain what will happen after we die, and what or where heaven is! We hear about it as a child as the place where God lives and where our loved ones go after they die. But where is it? Or to be more precise, what is heaven like? Much has been said, studied, and sought after regarding details about this unseen place. Movies try to depict it both in fiction stories such as in *Ghost* or *Casper*, or in non-fiction retellings such as *Heaven Is For Real*. We, as humans, try to capture with limited words and illustrations something that has yet to been seen or experienced by most, if not all of us. We want to know more, since the majority of us feel that heaven is our final destination after we leave the life we have now. Yet, most people fear death and the mystery of what lies beyond. Therein is the main purpose for this book, to dispel those fears by focusing on the joys that await us.

But prior to immersing ourselves in sweet thoughts about many of the pleasures to come in the hereafter, we need to recognize and deal with a few common obstacles that usually hinder our minds and imaginations when thinking about heaven. The first is confronting what we believe about an unseen spirit world around us. The second has to do with the validity of the major reference source for this book, the Bible. The third, and probably most cumbersome of the hindrances, is the inherent difficulty of human communication. If we recognize and conquer these obstacles, it will be easier to understand and believe what lies ahead of us after death. Think of these obstacles as the beginning of an amusement park ride. We buckle ourselves into the seat, feel the vehicle slowly start to move, and the momentum gradually builds up to that amazing point where anticipation is replaced with exhilaration. So let's buckle ourselves in and confront what we believe about the unseen world.

In order to understand what we will experience in a future heaven we need to understand that right now there are many things around us that are outside the limitations of our humanly vision. If we're to believe in heaven, it is imperative that we believe in what can't be seen with the human eye. For example, just as we can't actually see the wind, only the impact of the wind on earthly objects, there is a world around us that our physical eyes don't have access to...yet. But the day will come that "every eye shall see" (Revelation 1:7) what is currently unseen to those of us still walking and talking on this planet we call earth.

As for right now, there are some that say they have a connection to the intangible spirit world. Mediums reportedly can "hear" or "read" messages that the spirits of departed loved ones want to share with them. Although the Bible warns against the use of mediums (Leviticus 19:31, Deuteronomy 18), it does relate stories of Biblical leaders seeking the help of these "workers with familiar spirits" (1 Samuel 28, 2 Kings 21) much to the disapproval of God. And just as in almost every profession, there are some mediums who are imposters, who pretend to be able to communicate with the "other side" based on greed rather than a genuine ability. This leads to doubts about the authenticity of all of them. Just because some aren't legitimate, however, doesn't mean that all of them are illegitimate. There is plenty of evidence to support the ability of some people to actually communicate with the spirits of those who have died. Then there are others who aren't mediums who report having seen, and sometimes interacted with, the spirits of deceased loved ones. These experiences are usually when that person is alone and their heart is yearning for comfort due to the loss of the loved one. One such case is Zoey Mendoza.

In 2010, Zoey Mendoza's estranged husband brutally killed their two children, Jada and Jordan. About three weeks after their death Zoey, distraught and heartbroken, woke up one night to the sounds of her children laughing. She said the room was full of light even though it was still night time. She saw her smiling children standing upon a white staircase next to her bed. They came and briefly talked with her about heaven. Zoey went on to say that they still visit her occasionally through visions.

Then there is the recent news story from Utah about a mysterious voice leading rescuers to the place where a baby was trapped in an overturned car. A fisherman had found the wheels-up car partially submerged in the Spanish Fork River and alerted the authorities. According to the police officers that responded to the crash scene, they saw the car below the bridge that spans the river and heard an adult female voice saying "help me". After climbing down to the car, they found the lifeless body of mother Lynn Groesbeck but were surprised to see her baby still alive strapped in her upside down car seat. According to the evidence, Lynn had died upon impact over 12 hours earlier so where did the mysterious voice that those officers heard come from?

Aside from the "readings" of mediums, the stories of those who have seen visions of their loved ones, and the accounts of those who have witnessed the peaceful passing of the dying, there are countless testimonies of people who have received guidance through the "voice" of the Holy Spirit speaking to them. Although too numerous to include in this book, here are a few such examples that were sent to me. The first comes from Paula Frazier. She writes:

> "When I was younger, I bought a brand new 1977 Honda Civic Hatchback. I'd only had it a few short months when I started to experience a very loud, male voice while I was sleeping...not a dream, but, instead, a voice. Every single night for approximately six or seven nights in a row the "voice" would ask one question: "You know you don't have any brake lights don't you?" My answer was always "Yes!" Being a young female who knew literally nothing about cars other than the fact that they got you from point A to point B, I would have never suspected that a brand new car would have a problem with its brake lights. Each night when I would fall asleep, the same "voice" would ask me the same question, and, again, I would answer "Yes," yet not knowing why. This went on for many nights in a row. After about the sixth night in a row, I was telling my roommate about it on the way home from an evening out. I told her about the "voice" and the question it continued to ask me night after night. When we arrived back home, I asked her to do me a favor and check to see if I had any brake lights. It was found that I had no brake lights at all, and from that point on the voice was gone. I attribute the "voice" to the Holy Spirit who dwells within me, and has saved me from many dangers in my lifetime. Once He saw that I had finally taken heed of His message, He didn't have a need to ask the question any longer."

Another example comes from Erika Dolan from East Setauket, N.Y. who writes:

> "22 years ago I heard that voice telling me to go and get a colonoscopy and I ignored it the first time, I ignored that voice the second time but the third time the voice said you will die if you do not have a colonoscopy. The third time I listened and it turned out I had colon cancer. Someone, Holy Spirit, did not want me to die yet. It was not my time. When I got to the hospital for my operation I had a calmness about me which was odd. Not knowing what to expect, and not knowing if the cancer had spread you would think I would be a wreck. It was like I had an awareness that everything would be ok. Just before I was put under by the anesthesia the same voice said do not worry, everything will be ok now. I had the operation and needed no treatment other than being re-sectioned. You know it was strange that I knew what was being told to me but there was no voice like female or male. Just I knew what I was being told."

Sometimes the leading of the Holy Spirit isn't just for life and death reasons. Sometimes it is simply to guide us in decision making. Tom H. from Maryland shared one such example:

> "In 1993 I was transferred on my job to Key West Florida. My wife and son stayed behind to sell our house while I looked for a place to live on the other end. I was searching for a room to rent for a year until my family would be able to join me. I was in hotels for two weeks running up my credit card bill with no rooms available to rent. Every day I would check the

very small classifieds but never any rooms. I called my wife and told her I didn't know what to do because I couldn't afford it any longer. I was at a very low time being away from family and in a strange town with nowhere to live. I crossed all the classifieds out with a pen and lowered my head and was thinking of quitting my job and heading back home when a voice came to me and said, "Look at the paper again," very plainly. I looked and a number was there that said room to rent. I thought how did I miss this? But when I called the telephone number a woman answered the phone and said God knows you are hurting and wants to help you. She said I haven't the room but call this other number; they should have a room for you there. I did and a lady had an opening. When I got to the room the woman told me about on the phone, I had first bids because I came first. When I came out on the porch another woman was sitting there and asked me if I took the room. She told me her son was dying of cancer and she was looking for a room within walking distance of him since she had no car. I felt bad for her and she told me she had a room on hold at a different location 23 miles away but no transportation. So I paid it forward and gave her the room and drove 23 miles to the room she had previously reserved."

For those that still doubt the existence of a spirit world we can't see, there is more evidence in support of it from people who have witnessed the actual passing of someone else. There are many reports of people seeing the facial expression of a dying person change, in the last moments of life, to one of peace and pleasure. It's as if they are seeing something quite remarkable that those around them can't see. There are even reports of them uttering the names of loved ones long since gone, as if they are actually seeing and recognizing those that left this world prior to that time. Are some people able to see into the next world just prior to death? Are they able to see into heaven? It is strongly believed that that is exactly what those who were dying did see. So is there really an unseen spiritual world around us?

There are also numerous narratives in the Bible that support the existence of a supernatural world as well. Isaiah, Ezekiel, and Daniel wrote about what they saw in heaven. So did some of the apostles. More commonly known are the encounters many Biblical characters had with spiritual beings known as angels, who are usually unseen but appeared in human form at particular times to deliver messages from God. (Angel in Aramaic, the original language much of the Old Testament was written in, is malak, which means messenger or representative.) Just a few examples: angels appeared to Abram, Sarai, and Hagar in the book of Genesis, to Moses in Exodus, to Manoah and his wife in Judges, and to David in the books of Samuel and Chronicles. Then there are the stories from the New Testament of angels that appeared to Joseph, Mary, Zacharias, Peter, and John, as well as many others. Of course, the most well-known story of all that is often recited each year at Christmas time – the angels that appeared to the shepherds bringing the world's most amazing birth announcement. Each time these angels appeared they were delivering messages of comfort, caution, or direction.

Sometimes these spiritual beings did more than act as messengers though. They led the Israelites in Exodus, killed thousands in Isaiah and the second book of Samuel, shut the mouths of very hungry lions in the book of Daniel (we know they were very hungry due to their actions after Daniel was removed from their cage), and stirred the water of the Bethesda pool in John. They had other "supernatural" powers as well. An angel moved a huge boulder in Matthew and miraculously opened locked and guarded prison doors in Acts. There are many more accounts of the actions of these spirits we call angels that aren't listed here, but they did exist then and we have no reason to believe they don't still exist in our modern world. There are countless people alive today who testify about hearing words of warning or comfort from unseen beings.

In short, if we are going to believe in an invisible heaven we need to first believe that life in an invisible world does exist. There is evidence that an unseen world did exist many years ago, that it still exists today, and will continue to exist when this current visible world is wiped from our memories. After all, how can we believe in an unseen future world without acknowledging its existence in the past and present?

Looking Back to See Ahead

How would you feel if you were told that, after you die, you will still be able to not only walk and talk, but also sing and dance? What if you were told that your loved ones who have already died are able to do those exact things right now? Shocking, huh? Well, there's plenty of evidence in support of that belief. Sometimes though, in order for us to believe what will happen in the future, we need to look at the past. Or more importantly, we may feel we need to find reliable documentation from the past that we can lean on if we have doubts about future claims. For example, in the year 79 A.D. Mount Vesuvius erupted explosively and destroyed the neighboring city of Pompeii. It happened quickly and unexpectedly. How do we know that the destruction occurred so fast and so violently, rather than more gradually like with most volcanic eruptions? Besides some well-preserved ruins that were buried under a thick layer of ash, we also have written accounts from eye-witnesses. One of those witnesses was Pliny the Younger, a lawyer and magistrate of Ancient Rome, who recorded the details of the eruption in letters that were sent to his friend and historian Tacitus. Those letters still exist today and supported the belief that a similar massive volcanic event could happen again. So when Mount Saint Helens exploded in the northwestern United States in 1980, even though the resulting devastation was incredible, it wasn't entirely unbelievable due to what had been learned about the destructive power of other pyroclastic volcanoes, namely Mount Vesuvius, from those well-preserved ancient documents.

There are two points to be made from this. The first is that sometimes we can learn about future events by examining the written records of what people experienced many years ago. Good or bad, knowing what happened in the past can affect the choices we make about the future. What was learned about the speed of Vesuvius's destructive power has influenced where communities are built in respect to the proximity to suspected pyroclastic volcanos. The second point from the above story is that we have a tendency to believe eye-witness accounts more than just archeological evidence. Hearing about the pain and anguish of survivors from Pompeii made the event more realistic than simply observing the ash covered remains of the city. Those letters from Pliny the Younger deepened our understanding of what actually happened. They added intricate human details that would have only been speculation without them.

With those two points in mind from the Vesuvius example, let's look at an excerpt from another letter written around that same time by a physician named Luke to his friend, Theophilus, about an event that happened about 50 years before the destruction of Pompeii:

> "And it came to pass about eight days after these sayings, he took Peter and John and James, and went up into a mountain to pray. And as he prayed, the fashion of his countenance was altered, and his raiment was white and glistening. And, behold, there talked with him two men, which were Moses and Elias: Who appeared in glory, and spake of his decease which he should accomplish at Jerusalem. But Peter and they that were with him were heavy with sleep: and when they were awake, they saw his glory, and the two men that stood with him. And it came to pass, as they departed from him, Peter said unto Jesus,

Master, it is good for us to be here: and let us make three tabernacles; one for thee, and one for Moses, and one for Elias: not knowing what he said. While he thus spake, there came a cloud, and overshadowed them: and they feared as they entered into the cloud. And there came a voice out of the cloud, saying, This is my beloved Son: hear him. And when the voice was past, Jesus was found alone. And they kept it close, and told no man in those days any of those things which they had seen." (Luke 9:26-38)

Now, if we believe what Pliny wrote in his letters about Vesuvius, can't we also believe what Luke said happened in his? How is this letter from Luke similar to the letters from Pliny? The answer is simple. They are both eye-witness accounts of amazing events that happened many years ago *and* are both recorded on well-preserved ancient documents. Just as we gained deeper knowledge from Pliny of how a pyroclastic volcanic eruption can so swiftly and severely impact humans living near it, there is also much to be learned from Luke's letter to Theophilus about a world most of us won't see until after death. This is where the excitement begins!

So what evidence do we have that the spirits of our loved ones that have died can walk and talk? Look again at what Luke wrote. Those men that were there with Jesus saw Moses and Elias *standing* and *talking* with him! How exciting! If you don't understand why that is so amazing, keep in mind that Moses died at least 1200 years prior to this event and Elias (otherwise known as Elijah) had died at least 800 years earlier. Yet there they were, or should we say, there were their spirits, performing human acts in front of living witnesses. It should also be noted that Moses and Elias weren't sleeping either. They were awake and carrying on a conversation with Jesus.

The above letter from Luke and others like it are the historical foundation for what we know about what happens after we die. This is what was meant about needing to look back in order to see into our futures. There's so much more that we can learn from this particular letter and we'll refer back to it several times in later chapters. We'll also reference other letters in the Bible as well. The combination of modern testimonies such as those included in the first chapter and those eye-witness claims from many years ago give us a more solid launching pad from which to embark into the thrilling exploration of the new life ahead of us when we leave this one. Remember when I said this rollercoaster ride could get exciting? It most definitely will but we have a little more foundational work to do before the first breathtaking hill.

Limitations of Words

When I first felt led to write this book a song from the movie *The Sound Of Music* came to mind. In that movie, as the nuns were singing about the novitiate Maria they say, "How do you catch a cloud and pin it down?" This mirrored what I felt in trying to describe the indescribable. The main difficulty lies within the boundaries of our human communications. After unbelief in an unseen world, this is the second and largest obstacle we face when examining the topic of heaven. Today we use words, phrases, and sentences to share thoughts and ideas with another person, yet our very words can be very limiting. After all, how do you describe something that can't be seen, such as love, for example? It is easy to tell about what we <u>do</u> if we love someone but it is more difficult to actually tell what it <u>is</u> aside from it being an emotion. Love is a difficult topic to try to contain within the limits of human words just as the concept of heaven is.

Let's look at the problem of describing heaven a different way. Have you ever had very vivid detailed dreams, yet were unable to retell them to someone else exactly as you saw them later? Maybe in your dreams you were in places that were familiar to you in the dreams but not in reality. Home in the dream didn't look like the earthly home you have now or the one you remember as a child. You saw and talked with people in your dreams whom you knew in that context and were clear on what role they played in your life, but when you woke up they seemed either vague or possibly a compilation of several people. And in your dreams, have you ever been in one place and then were suddenly aware of being in a completely different place, sort of like a change of scene in a movie? Yet, how did you get from one place to another? In your dreams the event sequences make sense, but when awake they become jumbled and puzzling. These, as well other aspects of dreams, are difficult to describe to someone else let alone understand them yourself. These are the same problems we have when trying to describe with human language, an indescribable place like heaven. Sometimes words haven't been created that can convey the exact image we see or feeling we have. Our modern expansive dictionaries can be strangely very limiting.

Another problem with trying to describe heaven using mere human words is the words themselves. So many of our words have multiple meanings and uses. For example, look at how we use the words "hard" and "soft". On one hand, they are antonyms used as literal physical descriptions of animate objects i.e. the soft pillow was on the hard floor. On the other hand, the words hard and soft have been used to describe the figurative condition of someone's heart. A hard-hearted person is said to be unfeeling and a soft-hearted person is supposed to be kind and compassionate. But those two words can also be used to describe inanimate objects such as hard rock music and soft rock music. Some may feel that the two words are still being used as antonyms but in this case, are they truly antonyms since both are describing types of rock music? And how do you distinguish the difference between hard rock and soft rock to someone who is unable to hear? Which brings me back to the point…how do you use human words to confine a seemingly simple yet complex subject such as heaven? The limitations or complexity of trying to explain something such as heaven, using our limited human terminology, is almost impossible.

The next dilemma we face, when trying to answer questions regarding heaven, is the vastness of the topic. After all, trying to paint a clear picture of something we have never seen is similar to trying to describe God himself, who created heaven. As John Pavlovitz, a pastor/blogger from Wake Forest, North Carolina said, "The words in the Bible point to someone for whom words simply fail. The words are filled with good and lovely things that give us some frame of reference, but ultimately, God is far too big to be contained in those words." Pastor Pavlovitz goes on to explain this point using the ocean as an example. He said, "Billions of words have been written about the ocean. I could gather up every single one of them; the most beautiful, vivid, accurate descriptions from fisherman, marine biologists and poets. I could read every last word about the ocean to someone who has never been there—and it would never do it justice. There's simply no way to adequately describe the ocean in words. You have to experience it." The same is true about heaven. How do you give detailed answers to questions about heaven when you have never been there? This is, however, a mystery that I eagerly explored and now share what I've discovered with you. And even though what we know now about heaven may not be very clear, thankfully one day it will be. Or as Paul tells us in 1 Corinthians 13:12, we only have partial knowledge of God's infinite wisdom, but after death our knowledge will be complete.

Let me take a minute to underscore something I said earlier in the preface. It is up to the reader to decide what they believe or what they don't believe. Although Christians believe the Bible is the "inspired word of God", there are some topics within the Bible that are rather cloudy, or the center of much debate. For example, in the Old Testament, God tells us not to murder (Exodus 20:13), and in the New Testament, Jesus tells his disciples to not promote violence (Matthew 5). Yet we also see God instructing the Israelites to destroy every living thing in enemy villages, (1 Samuel 15) including women and children, and in Exodus we read of Moses murdering an Egyptian soldier without punishment from God. Pastor Pavlovitz explains this example of the Bible's vagueness like this - "That's why some Christians believe all violence is sinful, while others think shooting someone in self-defense is okay. Some find war justifiable in some cases, while some believe all war is inherently immoral. Same Bible. One subject. Several perspectives. That's not to say that truth is relative, that God doesn't have an opinion on violence or that He hasn't given us His opinion in the Bible. It's just that the answer may not be as clear and straightforward as we like to pretend it is. When you read and study this library (Bible) in its totality, there are certainly themes and continuities and things that connect exquisitely, but if we're honest we can also admit there are ambiguities. It doesn't diminish the Scriptures to admit that they are complex. On the contrary, most great works throughout history are."

The task of describing the indescribable has existed for thousands of years. The Old and New Testaments give witness to that. In the Old Testament, prophets like Jeremiah, Daniel, and Ezekiel used earthly words to describe heavenly visions. Some things were made very clear to them and were easier to relate to their audiences. Take Ezekiel for example. God gave him visions of what was to come if His chosen people didn't return to Him and Ezekiel relayed those visions to the people via language they understood. As one commentary puts it, "His style is plain and simple. His conceptions are definite, and the details even of the symbolical and enigmatical parts are given with lifelike minuteness. The obscurity lies in the substance, not in the form, of his communications. In his images he is magnificent, though austere and somewhat harsh. He abounds in repetitions, not for ornament, but for force and weight. His great aim was to stimulate the dormant minds of the Jews. For this end nothing was better suited than the use of mysterious symbols expressed in the plainest words." In other words, Ezekiel effectively combined common terminology of that time period with mysterious symbols to pass along a message to his intended audience.

Other visions in the Bible were more difficult to describe and so symbols were used to help illustrate or explain their visions, symbols that would have been familiar to their respective audiences. However, a problem lies within the use of those symbols for modern readers. What Ezekiel saw as a wheel in the sky in one of his visions and what our modern society pictures when they hear about a "wheel" in the sky may be starkly different. Was it similar to a chariot wheel or more like our modern interpretation of a flying saucer? Or what about John's description of the creatures that will torture people in the end times that don't have the "seal of God" on their foreheads? John describes them as being like "like horses made ready for war; and on their heads they had crowns like gold, and their faces were as the faces of men. And they had hair like the hair of women, and their teeth were as the teeth of lions. And they had breastplates like iron, and the sound of their wings was as the sound of carriages, like an army of horses rushing to the fight. And they have pointed tails like scorpions; and in their tails is their power to give men wounds for five months." (Revelation 9:7-10) We don't go to war with horses anymore, and most citizens haven't heard the sound made by the thundering hooves of a stampeding herd of animals. And what about those locusts having human faces, hair like women, and teeth like lion's teeth? The words used to describe what was seen by prophets in the Bible many years ago may not be the same words we would use to describe those same visions if we saw them today.

The point is that much of what is being described causes us to fill in the gaps with our own imaginations. We didn't see what the Biblical prophets saw or hear what they heard. And even if we had, would we struggle with trying to paint adequate verbal pictures just as the early prophets probably did? Even the Bible mentions the limitations earthly humans have in communicating compared to the spiritual realm. In the book of Romans we are told that that the Holy Spirit intervenes for us with Godly words outside of man's vocabulary. That indicates that there is a spiritual language beyond earthly understanding. We are also told that what is ahead of us is beyond our human imaginations. 1 Corinthians 2:9 says that what God has created for those that love Him goes beyond what anyone has ever seen or heard or imagined. So even though the Bible gives us some information regarding life beyond the here and now, describing heavenly matters is confined within our limited earthly language. We have been given some, but not all, of the intricate specifics of what heaven will look like, feel like, be like. We are told that those who are "saved" will look different in heaven but the exact details aren't known yet. Or as John says, when he's talking to other followers of Christ, that even though we are children of God it isn't clear "what we are to be." (1 John 3:2)

Please bear with me a little while longer while we look at one more example of how our earthly words can be such a stumbling block to our understanding of heaven and our anticipation of it here on earth. More specifically, the names we use when we are talking about heaven. The most common synonyms for heaven are the *city of God, Zion*, and *paradise*. This is where the seemingly simple gets a little more complex. According to most commentaries, in the Old Testament, the *city of God*, also called the city of David, is referring to God's earthly residence in Jerusalem and the holy temple. However, in the

New Testament, the term "city of God" is pointing to a place that hasn't become reality yet. It is the "new Jerusalem" that will be a part of the new heavens and new earth that God will bring about only AFTER the return of Jesus and our bodily resurrection. Since those events haven't happened yet, we don't have access to the city of God yet either. The name Zion, likewise, is used as a synonym for Jerusalem, both past and future. It refers to Mount Zion, a holy hill on which Jerusalem was located including the holy temple. However, the use of the word paradise as another name for heaven is where definitions divide.

There are many indications that there are two distinct places we refer to as heaven. As mentioned earlier, the eternal heaven, otherwise known as the *city of God* and "new heavens and new earth" don't exist yet because they will only come about AFTER Christ's return to this earth and the end time events specified in the Bible. The Bible does give some very specific and rather exciting details about that eternal heaven, but before we look at those in the Home Sweet Home chapter, we need to look at what it says about the third heaven since most, if not all, of us will encounter it first. And for the sake of clarity, we'll continue to refer to it as the third heaven, or temporary heaven, as opposed to the eternal heaven, which will be ever grander than our temporary heavenly abode directly after death.

Finally, although thought to have similar meanings, the terms *paradise* and the *city of God* have distinct differences. Again, one is temporary while the other is eternal. This is where the discussion about heaven can be both confusing and exciting. The word *paradise* is only used three times in the King James Version of the Bible and, all three times, it is referring to a place other than the eternal *city of God*. As one Bible dictionary explains it, paradise is "the part of Hades which was thought by the later Jews to be the abode of the souls of the pious until the resurrection: but some understand this to be a heavenly paradise the upper regions of the heavens. According to the early church Fathers, the paradise in which our first parents dwelt before the fall still exists, neither on the earth nor in the heavens, but above and beyond the world." This is what is also referred to as the "third heaven" by Paul in 2 Corinthians 12.

Remember when I said this rollercoaster ride could get exciting? We're finally at the summit of this thrilling ride! Use your mind's eye to see ahead of you seven joy-inducing loops, or sections of the track, with each hopefully adding to the anticipation of your final destination and taking away any dread or doubt about what lies beyond the veil of death. The six chapters ahead aren't in any particular order, but there is one division that needs to be noted. The first three chapters are mainly concerned with what can be expected immediately after death but before Christ's return, otherwise referred to as the third heaven or temporary heaven. The latter chapters will focus more specifically on what we can look forward to after the *city of God* that is described in the book of Revelations will be brought down to earth, what will be referred to as the eternal heaven. And there are some heavenly perks that can be expected in both the temporary third heaven and the eternal heaven; therefore there is some crossover in a few of the chapters. But whichever way you look at it, they are all going to be out of this world and absolutely to die for (bad puns intended). So are you ready to leave this slightly tedious but necessary part of the book and launch into some breathtaking, possibly mind-boggling glimpses into what awaits us after death?! Hold on tight and remember to keep your mind's eye open in order to better see what we can look forward to in the lifetime ahead. And away we go!

No Pain All Gain (or Retirement In Heaven)

The first thrilling reason not to fear death is... (drum roll please) ...freedom from pain. That may sound rather simplistic but let's try to get a bigger, more detailed picture of what that will entail.

On this earth we are subject to many types of pain. I think it is safe to say that all of us have had to endure a dizzying array of physical ailments throughout our lifetime. The physical pain can range from an annoying splinter in a finger to whole body traumas, such as some experience as the result of automobile accidents or other horrific events. On the spectrum between those two extremes are headaches, neck injuries, back pain, broken bones, heartburn, stomach aches, joint pain, and various infections and diseases. Every part of our earthly body is subject to possible painful maladies. That's the bad news. Now for the good news seasoned with a little humor.

News flash – heaven's going to be filled with retired folks! Yes, you read that right. So you may be asking, "How is that good news?" and "What does that have to do with there not being any pain in heaven?" The answer is simple. Everyone on this earth that has a career related to the medical field will receive automatic retirement benefits in heaven. Why? Revelation 21:4 tells us that God will wipe away all tears from His children; and that there will be no more death, sorrow, or crying. There also won't be any more pain. (Even though this verse describes what the eternal heaven will be like, in a sense it also applies to us in the temporary heaven. Yes, many of the jobs that are currently held on this earth won't be needed in the city of God, as will be highlighted in Chapter 9, but they also won't be needed in the temporary heaven either.) After death we will be free from the earthly bodies that were so easily beset with injury and illness.

Not having a susceptible earthly body means freedom from earthly maladies and pain. How wonderful it will be to never need the services of doctors and nurses again! Let's savor that verse even more by slowing down and taking it apart. The best way to do that is to look at the Greek meanings of some of the key words in that promise, since that is the original language in which it was written.

First are the words *death* and *sorrow*. In Greek, *death* is "thanatos" which is defined as "the death of the body i.e. that separation (whether natural or violent) of the soul and the body by which the life on earth is ended" and "penthos" which is Greek for mourning. Simply put, there will be no more death and the heartbreak that results. There will also be no more "ponos" which means great trouble or pain. Think about that for a minute. The viruses and bacteria that exist on this earth that cause so much misery will be excluded from heaven. There won't be any need for antibacterial soap, antibiotics, or antiviral medicines. So besides the non-necessity of medical staff in heaven, there won't be pharmacies and pharmacists, mortuaries or morticians. There won't be pharmaceutical companies or drug stores, hospitals or rehab facilities. In heaven we'll be free from all pain and illness. On top of all that, the Greek word for *eyes* is "ophthalmos" which not only refers to the literal human eyes but also the metaphorical eyes of the mind. Thus not only will we be free from physical pain but also from mental anguish, emotional heartache, and depression. Stress, gone. Worry, nonexistent. Anxiety, absent. So, added to the heavenly retirement list will be therapists, psychiatrists, and psychologists.

There's even more good news, especially for those who enjoy hearty helpings of laughter. See back up there in the verse where we are told that God will wipe away all tears? The Greek word for *all* is "pas" which translated means "each, every, any, all". Or, as a favorite pastor used to say, "All means all." Hence, all sources for tears, both good and bad, possibly won't exist. Laughing until crying may be impossible. Evidently, we'll be able to laugh as much as we want for as long as we want without any accompanying sore smile muscles either. A small perk but a perk none the less, especially for those who thoroughly enjoy laughing until it hurts. But the good news doesn't stop there.

The apostle Paul clued us in on another sweet aspect of heaven when he said Jesus will change our corrupted bodies into glorified bodies like His own. (Philippians 3:21) What does that mean? We get to have glorified bodies like Jesus' resurrected body! We will have bodies that don't get tired and worn out, that don't need to reenergize through sleeping. Have you ever wondered why God created day and night? Could it be that He knew that these earthly bodies "made of clay" would need time to rest after working or playing hard during the day? One of the many curiosities about these earthly human bodies is the amount of time it requires to reenergize after being active. Most medical research states that for optimal health, children through school age need to spend about half of a 24-hour day sleeping, and that adults should devote around 1/3 of their day to sleep, or 7-8 hours. Translated, that means that we spend at least 1/3 of our earthly lifetime sleeping! In other words, if we live to be 60 years old we will have spent 20 years asleep! Is that one reason God created nighttime, because He knew how easily these bodies would tire and therefore created an environment that was more conducive to resting? If so, what will it be like to have glorified bodies that won't need to spend so much time sleeping?

There's another sweet morsel of truth in that verse as well. Think about a couple of the amazing physical feats Jesus was able to do. He walked on water (John 6:19) and walked through walls or locked doors (John 20). In short, there were no physical barriers that prevented the resurrected Jesus from traveling to wherever He wanted. We'll be able to do the same thing. We'll be able to go anywhere we want, unencumbered by doors, walls, rivers, or mountains. Hence, and humorously, the list of those with permanent retirement in heaven dramatically increases due to the unnecessary modes of transportation that we have here on earth. Say bye-bye to stuffy crowded planes, trains, and automobiles. We'll be able to stroll tirelessly through the realms of heaven without the assistance of manmade conveyance contraptions. So those of you that are in any way connected to our earthly transportation systems, get ready to enjoy your eternal retirement rewards.

Let's add an additional physical perk our glorified bodies will have in heaven that we currently don't have down here – x-ray vision. No, not the ability to see through objects like certain cartoon characters supposedly can. In heaven we'll be able to see the unseen spiritual world that currently exists around us. As mentioned in Chapter One, there is another realm that presently surrounds us that our human eyes very rarely, if ever, get to see. It is the spiritual domain that consists of angels and the spirits of those who have crossed over from this life to the next. There are many instances in the Bible of man seeing angels and even the spirits of people that have previously died. Some of those will be discussed in the next chapter about reunions in heaven. For now, here's a couple of eye opening accounts (pun intended) from the Bible in which men and even a donkey got to see into the unseen world.

The first is of the prophet Elisha and his servant who got to see "guardian angels" first hand. God repeatedly showed Elisha, one of His prophets, what the king of Aram and his army was about to do so that Elisha could forewarn the king of Israel. The king of Aram became "greatly troubled" and thought he had a traitor within his household. When his servants informed him that it wasn't a traitor but instead it was the prophet Elisha who seemed to know the king's plans ahead of time, the king sent his servants to go find him. They reported back to the king that Elisha was in the city of Dothan. Upon learning of this the king of Aram sent his army to surround Dothan. Seeing the town surrounded Elisha's servant became very afraid and asked Elisha what they should do. Elisha calmly told him not to be afraid because God's army outnumbered the king's army. Then he prayed and asked God to let the servant see the unseen. God did and the servant saw what Elisha had already seen, the mountain "full of horses and carriages of fire". 2 Kings 6:11-17

This second example has an additional element of awe in that not only does man see into the "heavenlies" but also an animal and that animal is given the ability to talk. The central figure in this narrative is Balaam, someone who acknowledged God's authority and power but wasn't one of "God's chosen people". He practiced divination, meaning he interpreted signs and omens, but was greedy and willing to obey God's commands as long as he was going to profit from doing so. Therefore when the king of Moab became fearful of the approaching Israelites, who had recently defeated two other kingdoms, asked Balaam to go with his army to help them defeat the Israelites Balaam tells the king's messengers that he can't go because God warned him in a dream not to. The king of Moab then sends more influential ambassadors to try to entice Balaam with even more money. Balaam chooses to defy God's command and begins to follow after the Moabite entourage on his donkey. So God sends an angel to block the donkey's path. Balaam can't see the angel who is holding up a sword but the donkey can and goes off of the road into a field. This angers Balaam and he beats the animal, forcing it onto a narrow path with walls on either side of it. Again the angel appears before the donkey and, trying to avoid what Balaam can't see, it pushes up against one of the walls crushing one of Balaam's feet. Now even angrier, Balaam beats the donkey again and forces it onto an even narrower path. For the third time the angel appears and, being unable to turn around, the donkey lies down. Filled with fury, Balaam again beats the animal. Suddenly God allowed the donkey to speak at which point the donkey asks Balaam why he was being beaten. Balaam replied that it was because the donkey had "mocked" him and that if he had had a sword he would have killed it. Then God "opened the eyes of Balaam" and he saw what was previously unseen, the sword wielding angel, leading him to fall on his face and confess his greed and rebellion and agree to not go after the Moabites. (Numbers 22)

What is amazing in this story is not just that a human was able to see into the angelic realm, but that an animal was too. Based on this narrative, we learn that animals are also sometimes given the ability to see what is unseen. Let's take this a step further. Could this be the reason why Noah didn't have to gather the animals into the ark he built but rather they came by themselves? Were they being shepherded by unseen beings? This is something else that can be pondered on as we relish the idea of there being a spectacular world around us that we'll finally be able to see when we leave this life.

And while we're on the topic of vision, how sweet will it be for those who currently don't have 20/20 eyesight to have perfect vision in heaven? Those that are blind on this earth will see beauty beyond imagination. Those down here who have difficulty seeing for whatever reason will be able to view the wonders of heaven in minute detail. There won't be a need for eyeglasses, opticians, or ophthalmologists. And since God will be the source of light in heaven we won't have to protect our eyes from the damaging rays of the sun. If we stare at the sun now it destroys our eyes, but God's light is brighter than the sun and doesn't damage our eyes. Therefore we won't need sunglasses, wide-brimmed hats, or ball caps to shield our eyes from the harshness of the sun. So if you presently have to squint when you step outside on a sunny day, take comfort in knowing that when you leave your heavenly mansion to stroll around heaven, you won't have to be concerned about where you left your shades.

While we're enjoying the thought of having glorified bodies in heaven, here's one of the most delicious morsels yet - there won't be any need for the huge medical device manufacturers in heaven that we have here on earth. Why? Because our heavenly bodies will be free from any physical defects, deformities, or disorders. From autism to club feet, deafness to paralysis, from the tops of our heads to the tips of our toes and every body part in between, our new bodies will be free from any and all earthly imperfections. The twisted human bodies that presently confine such beautiful spirits within them will be dropped like unwanted garments to never be picked up again. Wheelchairs, walkers, and electronic devices these precious souls are dependent on while on this planet will be discarded like distasteful debris. The loved ones who are left behind will be able to look at those objects with a measure of unexpected joy knowing their loved ones above are walking, talking, and singing unrestrained by those clunky gadgets. Now there's something to rejoice about!

Another career field that will be nonexistent in the "realms above" is the security industry. Since there is no sin in heaven ("For he that is dead is freed from sin" Romans 6:7) the need for protection from the results of sinful actions will be unnecessary too. So the ranks of the retired grow exponentially. Why? Not only will locksmiths, gunsmiths, and alarm manufacturers be able to retire the tools of their trades, so will all of those currently employed in the protection of homes, cities, and countries. Meaning all members of police and fire departments, as well as all members of all branches of the military will be able to hang up their hats, put their feet up, and simply enjoy their heavenly retirement.

Lastly, there is one more "industry" related to earthly physical comfort that may be noticeably absent in heaven. (Hopefully the fashionistas that are reading this are sitting down.) We're told in the last book of the Bible that, "He that overcometh, the same shall be clothed in white raiment; and I will not blot out his name out of the book of life, but I will confess his name before my Father, and before his angels." (Revelation 3:5) Translation - we'll all be wearing robes and the "in" color will be white. Ok, maybe our heavenly attire won't be robes per se, as is often what is depicted in art and literature. However, the Greek word for raiment is "himation" which is defined as "a garment (of any sort)" and "the cloak or mantle and the tunic". And since comfort is one of the primary themes of heavenly living it stands to reason that what we will be wearing in heaven won't have tight collars, uncomfortable waistbands, and complicated closures. On top of that the Bible is very clear about the color – white, white, and more white since white signifies righteousness. If it's good enough for the angels (John 20:12), it is good enough for us. Besides, Jesus said in Matthew 6, "And why are ye anxious concerning raiment? Consider the lilies of the field, how they grow; they toil not, neither do they spin: yet I say unto you, that even Solomon in all his glory was not arrayed like one of these." Can you imagine that? Our heavenly wardrobe will be beautifully white like lilies that were more breath-taking than a king's robes! So besides all the other careers that won't be needed in heaven, everyone that has an earthly job that is in anyway related to the fashion industry and the marketing thereof can start planning their eternal retirement party too.

Now, if one of your earthly passions is fashion and you're lamenting the limited wardrobe choices in heaven, there is a piece of good news about our heavenly apparel that may be especially thrilling for you. We will be given an amazing accessory to wear with our comfortable white robes, namely a crown. In Revelations 2:10 it is called "the crown of life" and in 2 Timothy 4:8 it is called "a crown of righteousness". So amidst the extensive retirement rolls in heaven, there might be skilled artisans joyfully helping in a tiara factory or crown company. Either way, our crowns will symbolize our victory over death, so we should wear it happily atop our angelic heads.

Dear readers, do aches and pains currently rob you of earthly joy? Do you have concerns about earthly comforts? Then be encouraged by these words from Paul. "For I reckon that the sufferings of this present time are not worthy to be compared with the glory which shall be revealed in us." (Romans 8:18) The word *glory* is explained by one theological dictionary as "the glorious condition of blessedness into which is appointed and promised that true Christians shall enter after their Savior's return from heaven". Sounds pretty good, huh?

Reunions And Rock Stars

Have you ever been asked the hypothetical question, "If you could invite any 5 people to dinner, famous or not, living or dead, who would you invite?" Seems like a fanciful question with improbable guests. After all, how many people really get to meet the famous people they look up to? On top of that, it's impossible to actually have a "meet and greet" with well-known historical figures that died many years ago. Or is it? That may be true on this earth at this present time, but guess what? In heaven, you'll not only be able to share a meal with those select few but with many others as well. The guest list won't have to be limited to 5, and more importantly, death will no longer be an obstacle to spending time face-to-face with those who died before us. How do we know this? First, let's look at the seventeenth chapter of the book of Matthew.

In this account, Jesus takes three of his apostles, Peter, James, and John, up onto a tall mountain with him. There he is transfigured before their eyes into his glorified body with his face and clothing becoming radiant. The apostles then see into the unseen world and witness Jesus talking with Moses and Elias. So Peter tells Jesus that they are privileged to be witnesses of this meeting and asks if he and the other apostles can build shelters for Jesus, Moses, and Elias. They're then enveloped with a bright cloud from which God speaks.

Here we see that a handful of Jesus's apostles witness him talking with Moses and Elias after they had sought seclusion on a mountain to pray. Exactly what they talked about isn't known but one version of the story, as retold by Luke (as was referenced in Chapter 2 of this book), says that they talked about the upcoming death of Jesus. Can you imagine that conversation? Then there is the question about how long the three of them were standing around talking. According to Luke's version, the apostles that were with Jesus became very sleepy. Was this because of the arduous climb up the mountain or the extended conversation they were eavesdropping on, or maybe a combination of both? Either way how many of us would have stared in starry-eyed wonder at these two historical heavy-hitters with our mouths gaping open and with minds full of questions? Now, imagine being able to visit with each of them, one on one, and ask any and all questions that come to mind. Would you go from asking questions like an eager newspaper reporter to laughing at the many humorous anecdotes each of them could share with you?

Let's go one step further and imagine relaxing in a beautiful, well-lit heavenly room that is furnished with incredibly plush, comfortable recliners that are positioned in a circle, facing each other, and in those chairs are family and friends whom you loved deeply on the earth. Can you imagine the stories that would be told, and the abundant giggles and laughter repeatedly being heard by other citizens of heaven nearby? Many of us have had a foretaste of these jovial gatherings while living here below. Maybe it was when we were sitting around a campfire or picnic table. Or maybe it was with friends at a party or with family at a reunion. Now take that memory and subtract the sore muscles from laughing or smiling too much and add the breathtaking scenery of your choosing. You can grin with grandparents, chuckle with your children, snicker with siblings, and guffaw with various other family members. But you don't have to stop there. You can cavort with classmates, frolic with friends, and chuckle with chums. Get the picture?

If you think those scenarios sound good, we need to enlarge the image. Have you ever thought about how many people you have encountered in your own singular lifetime? Go all the way back to childhood. Were there best friends from elementary school whom you shared special times with? Do you ever wonder what happened to them after you grew up and moved away from each other? In heaven you'll be able rekindle old friendships and swap stories of adventures you each separately experienced. What about those teenage friends that you shared adolescent angsts with? Or dear neighbors that waved from front porches and gave you sweet treats on holidays? The more you think about it the more people that will probably come to mind. What will it be like to see them again? What will you talk about? Memory lane in heaven might be endless.

Another sweet aspect about the reunions in heaven goes beyond the earthly relationships that brought us much joy and happiness. There will also be healing for broken relationships. In heaven our focus will be on God's righteousness, not our own "rightness". Therefore all those mingling in the great out-there will set aside the issues that caused the breakdown of earthly relationships and be bonded through the common love of Christ. As He said in the book of Luke, "My mother and my brothers are those who have knowledge of the word of God and do it." We won't be hurt by others nor will we be able to cause anyone else pain. We'll become a very close-knit family with heavenly healing abounding.

Heaven isn't just going to be about earthly family and friends reuniting though. It is even better than that, as hard as that may be to imagine. Let's just suppose that while you're strolling through that third heaven, you come across another group of people whom you have never met, but strangely enough you recognize. Maybe it's those five famous people from the hypothetical question at the beginning of this chapter. It could be Holy Rock Stars such as Abraham, King David, Daniel, Joshua, and Jesus himself. Maybe it's Constantine the Great, Johannes Gutenberg, Christopher Columbus, Leonardo da Vinci, and Martin Luther. Or maybe it's Martin Luther King, Mother Teresa, Eva Burrows, C.S. Lewis, and J.R.R. Tolkien. So many holy heavy hitters to choose from! Yet how will we know them if we have never met them? People with deeply analytical minds may reason that those famous persons named above who lived within the last century may be easier to identify due to there being photos or paintings of them here on earth. But what about those "holy rollers" that we don't have manmade representations of? We'll recognize them the same way Peter, James, and John recognized Moses and Elias who had died many hundreds of years before that mountaintop encounter. We'll just know. That is one of the hard to imagine but miraculously wonderful realities of living in heaven. How amazing is that?!

It gets even better though. Have you ever thought about exactly WHAT you will talk about while mingling with all these heavenly sojourners? The topics are seemingly limitless due to the great variety of generations that will be represented in heaven. For example, some of us are old enough to have had parents or grandparents that lived during a time when electricity wasn't a standard component of every house, especially in rural areas. We knew this usually because they shared what life was like for them prior to having access to it. They, in turn, may have been told stories by their parents and grandparents about what it was like immigrating to a foreign country, quite possibly by way of a boat or ship. And so on and so on. Each generation has passed on stories about what their early life was like. We'll be able to learn about history from the actual primary sources, those that lived through particular time periods in particular cultures. If we want to know more about what it was like to live during the Ming Dynasty in China, the Middle Ages in Europe, or in the Ptolemaic Kingdom in Africa, we'll be able to inquire directly from the former residents themselves. Can you even begin to imagine eavesdropping on the conversations of groups of heavenly citizens that are composed of a mixture peoples from various time periods? Interesting doesn't begin to describe it.

There's one more sweet tidbit about our fellowship time in heaven. When we get there we will be welcomed by a mind-boggling cheering section. We get a peek at that celebration in the book of Hebrews. The first verse of the twelfth chapter says, "Wherefore seeing we also are compassed about with so great a cloud of witnesses, let us lay aside every weight, and the sin which doth so easily beset us, and let us run with patience the race that is set before us." The word for cloud in Greek is "nephos" which translated means a large dense multitude, or a throng. Therefore we know that right now there is a throng of heavenly witnesses waiting at the finish line cheering us on and waiting to welcome us to our heavenly home. Let's take a closer look at that for a minute.

If you were to write down all the people you are friends with, or have personally known in your lifetime, how many people would be on that list? Several hundred maybe? Or possibly several thousand? How many people are you connected with on the various social media sites? Now imagine that many people, and even more, are watching as you are "running" in this earthly race and then as you reach the end. Now add to that list of your pious pep club the aforementioned heavenly "holy rollers" and the rock stars of heaven. Can you see them cheering and clapping and eager to hug you as you cross that heavenly finish line? If you listen very carefully maybe you can even hear them.

Let's let this thought of a heavenly cheering section sink in even deeper. When you were younger were you ever nervous on the first day of school, wondering if there would be any familiar friendly faces to greet you and make you feel loved and accepted? Or maybe it was getting on a bus looking for a place to sit, hoping someone would invite you to sit next to them? If so, remember how good it felt to see the welcoming smile of a classmate or companion? Now multiply that feeling many times over. When you cross that finish line into heaven you will be instantly surrounded with smiling friendly faces and more hugs and "high-fives" than you could have imagined here on earth. No earthly cheering section can compare to what awaits us in heaven. And who will be up front and center waiting to greet you? The seventh chapter of the book of Acts holds the answer to that question. "'But Stephen, being full of the Holy Ghost, looked up steadfastly into heaven, and saw the glory of God, and Jesus standing on the right hand of God, And said, Behold, I see the heavens opened, and the Son of man standing on the right hand of God.'" How absolutely wonderful will that be!

Being able to have unlimited conversations, confabs, and chats with Christians who we weren't able to during our earthly lifetimes or with loved ones who have gone ahead of us is just one of the perks awaiting us in heaven. With this in mind, let your mind wander for a while and ponder about whom you would like to talk to and what topics you would like to talk with those heavenly citizens about. After all, since God is the only one with infinite knowledge and wisdom, there will be plenty to talk about and plenty of people to talk to. There is space at the back of the book to jot down some of those that come to mind. Does that sound like an unusual request for a non-fiction book? Remember, the purpose of this book is to ease the fear of death. Can you think of a nicer way to conquer that fear than focusing on the fellowships we'll have when we finally get there? The other reasons included in this book may be sweet, but creating and renewing relationships seems to be the most popular answer in numerous research polls about life after death. So go ahead, write down whom you are looking forward to seeing when you get to heaven. Make it real by putting it in writing. Include topics of conversation if you want. For example, have you ever wondered what Jesus' childhood was like? Or maybe you just want to excitedly share a lot of "guess what's" and "remember when's". If so, write them down. There are fabulous times of fellowship ahead so don't let current circumstances or concerns hinder your list. Keep in mind this isn't a "wish" list, it's a "want" list. Heaven is real and so will be our reunions with relatives and powwows with the pious. How great is that going to be?!

Eternity Is A Good Thing

Have you ever had the privilege of going on a vacation away from home for a week or more? Think about all the earthly effort that it took to accomplish it. First, you probably had to save up the money for it which may have taken months or even years. Then came the planning phase that may have included internet searches, referrals from friends, and making hotel reservations, as well as securing modes of transportation. Days may have been marked off on a calendar in anticipation of the day of departure. Lastly, before leaving, there may have been lists checked of what was supposed to be packed, arrangements made for pets that were going to be left behind, and double-checking that appliances were turned off and the home was secure. Your efforts didn't stop there though.

Upon arriving at your intended destination after a lengthy car or plane ride, there was probably a short unwritten to-do list that included some unpacking, eating a meal, and a brief investigation of the immediate area. Then the fun-filled, jam-packed schedule of activities began. You wanted to be able to see and do as much as possible within the time-limits of your well-deserved vacation. Soon the days filled with scurrying around had you exhausted and you just wanted to relax. But before you knew it, it was time to begin packing suitcases again for the return trip home. After another lengthy ride home you lugged bags and souvenirs through the front door where they were dropped. The realities of being home sunk in with a thud as you thought about the growing list of chores that needed to be done like unpacking dirty clothes, doing the laundry, fetching boarded pets, retrieving unopened mail, and planning what to eat. You also realized that within what seemed like a few short hours you would be back at work and your well-planned, much anticipated vacation would all too quickly be a distant memory. You looked around you and fatigue enveloped you as you wish you had a vacation from your vacation. Months of saving, planning, and preparation resulted in an enjoyable but quickly over get away that had left your bank account and your body drained.

Time for another wonderful reason not to fear death by looking at that vacation from a heavenly perspective. What if, instead of just a week or two to explore and enjoy one specific destination, you had an eternity to do so? Instead of cramming as much activity as you could into a limited amount of time, you were able to take as much time as you would like to go visit a place. And remember those vacations where, once you were there, you discovered even more things you wanted to go see and do but your schedule was already filled to capacity? In heaven that won't be a problem. You'll have limitless time to go and see and do. You will have no schedules to fill, no deadlines to meet, no agendas to be confined to. You can visit any heavenly splendor you want for as long as you want whenever you want. Your adventures won't be overshadowed with a sense of urgency or a dread of them ending.

Here's another way to look at it. Have you ever known anyone who had a season pass to a local tourist attraction such as an amusement park or a zoo? These passes usually allow for unlimited visits to that specific attraction within a given amount of time, customarily for a calendar year or during the days they are open in that particular year which is referred to as a "season". By having a season pass the owners of that pass aren't pressured to do as much as possible within a single visit. Each day trip to that specific venue is probably more relaxed because they are going to only focus on one part of the park or zoo at a time. They don't feel like they have to "enjoy themselves to exhaustion" with each visit. That is what heaven will be like. The big difference though is that your heavenly season pass never expires. Jesus said that whoever puts their trust in Him they will have eternal life. (John 6:47)

With that in mind, have you ever thought about how confined we are by time limits here on earth? Some cellphone packages come with restrictions on the amount of talk time you have, projects at work can have specific deadlines, and most salaried employees are expected to work a minimum number of hours in order to justify their paycheck. If you work for an hourly wage you are usually told when you have to clock in and when you have to clock out. Can you imagine what it would be like to live in a place where there aren't any clocks or watches that dictate our actions?

Strangely enough, time is a concept that man didn't create but has tried to harness, codify, classify, and control from almost the beginning of his existence. We get fixated on it, sometimes even to the point of obsessing over it. We try to cram as much chosen "busyness" activities into it as we think we can all the while sacrificing other activities that we deem less important such as sleep or rest. On earth, time is either our enemy or our friend. We either embrace it or rail against it. But what exactly is it? We know it is an unseen "thing" that can neither be touched nor contained, such as the wind. But like the wind we can see the evidence of it moving. Plants sprout, grow, blossom, fruit, wither, shrivel, and decompose, all in the span of an earthly season or two. Mountains and hills slowly erode under the forces of wind and weather over the course of centuries and millenniums. And somewhere in between, humans are born, thrive, explore, conquer, yield, and then retire within the brackets of mere decades. Some think that "time marches on" as broadcaster Westbrook Van Voorhis often stated. Still others agree with Henry Austin Dobson's sentiment in his poem The Paradox of Time that "Time goes, you say? Ah no! Alas, Time stays, we go"; that we humans are the ones moving through time, that we are travelers along a static timeline.

Whatever definition you choose to use to describe time, think about what it would be like if it didn't exist. Currently our seasons are created by the earth's rotation around the sun, and days and nights are differentiated by the existence of or lack of sunshine. We have even figured out how to divide daytime and nighttime into smaller and smaller segments called hours, minutes, and seconds. Just take a minute (pardon the pun) to look around you right now and count how many devices you have that remind you what time it is. Calendars, clocks, watches, and cellphones are usually within our sight, if not within our reach, everywhere we go. But what will it be like if there is no sun or moon to divide our heavenly days in half? Will we even miss not being able to know exactly what time it is? So here's a humorous thought to ponder. If time is eternal in heaven, will it be possible to be late for anything? If not, then those of us who are plagued with an earthly fear of being late can take a deep sigh of relief.

On a side note, there was reportedly a church pastor who supposedly said one of his concerns about spending eternity heaven was being bored. According to him, the thought of doing the same things over and over for infinity was frightening. This would be an understandable fear if being in heaven were similar to sitting in a lengthy meeting or conference that was at first interesting, but quickly became tedious or boring. Most of us have endured at least one of those in our lifetime. In this scenario we find ourselves repeatedly looking at our watch or cellphone and doodling on whatever paper we have handy, all the while counting the minutes until we can escape, er, leave. However, heaven has a different "clock" or time measurement than we do on earth. God doesn't measure time in human terms. Peter tells us that to God one day is like one thousand years and one thousand years are like a day. (2 Peter 3:8) So those who died a thousand or so years ago, according to our human calendars, have really only been there a minute or two by God's wristwatch. In other words, if we have a loved one that passed away within our lifetimes, by God's standard of time measurement, they just arrived. Our earthly perspective of time and the heavenly perspective of time are vastly different. So if we look at the death of our loved ones from heaven's viewpoint, they haven't even had enough heavenly time to find their seat at that great meeting in the sky, let alone have time to get bored. Randy Alcorn, in his book *Heaven*, addressed the issue of boredom in heaven another way. He said, "God promises that we'll laugh, rejoice, and experience endless pleasures in Heaven. To be in His presence will be the opposite of boredom. Once we're with the Lord, the only boring place in the universe will be Hell."

Time here on earth is treasured simply because, like rare metals and precious gemstones, it is limited in number or quantity. As American entrepreneur and author Jim Rohn once said, "Time is more valuable than money. You can get more money, but you cannot get more time." So when we get to heaven and time is limitless, will it become as unimportant as gold will be? Think back to those heavenly reunions we pondered in the last chapter. There will potentially be thousands and thousands of loved ones, friends, and new faces to have eternal "meet and greets" and gab sessions with. Timelessness will be a blessing, not a curse.

In a letter to the Corinthians, Paul says that when our earthly bodies die we are given an eternal heavenly body. (2 Corinthians 5:1) On earth, time is often our enemy. It confines our actions and dictates our schedules. The good news is that in the world to come, time becomes our friend. Rather than confining us, it frees us. Rather than dictating to us, it delights us. Death removes all hindrances and burdens of time. Or as author William Faulkner once said, "Only when the clock stops does time come to life." Time may "march" here on earth but if the old adage "Time flies while you're having fun" is true, then in heaven time is going to take flight.

Traveling Light (or More Heavenly No-no's)

Sometimes, what takes a trip from being good to great is what ISN'T a part of the vacation. Remember the scenario from the beginning of the last chapter? Well, let's unpack it even more starting with the preparations prior to leaving. In doing so we'll take a closer look at some of the animate, as well as the inanimate objects that won't be in your heavenly suitcases.

First, as was pointed out in earlier, our heavenly wardrobe will be supplied upon departure from this earth. Comfortable white robes, better than any you might find at earthly luxury resorts, will be ready for you. When you drop this "robe of flesh" you will be given a "robe of righteousness". Therefore your luggage should be almost empty at this point. But there are a few more items that we can discard too.

Remember from the last chapter all the preparations that were required in the weeks and months leading up to your earthly vacation departure? The biggest hindrance that had to be overcome was probably the budget. You probably had to save up money which may have taken months or even years. Then came the making of hotel reservations, as well as securing modes of transportation. Before you left on your vacation, you may have printed off lodging and transportation confirmations, and possibly even your airline tickets. You may have prepaid for some things, but you also needed to take along some form of currency, maybe a combination of cash and credit cards. Well, the trip you are going on to heaven is an all-expense paid, all-inclusive dream come true trip. Romans 6:23 says that the payment for sin is death but that God offers eternal life <u>freely</u> through His son Jesus. The price for admission has already been paid and your lodging, which will be discussed in the next chapter, is already being prepared for your arrival. Therefore no money in any form is needed on this eternal vacation. You can chuck your checkbook, discard your credit and debit cards, and cast aside your cash.

On your heavenly trip you also won't have to keep track of passports, hotel confirmations, or plane tickets. According to Revelation 3:5, those that overcome this world will be dressed in white and God will not erase their name from the book of life. Did you see it right there? All the documentation you will need for your admission to heaven is already there waiting for you. If you are an "overcomer" your name is written in the best book ever created, the book of life. (The Greek word for overcometh is "nikao" which means "those that hold fast to their faith even unto death against the power of their foes, temptations and persecutions".) That will be so much more valuable than having your name etched into a headstone or written on a death certificate. And there's one more precious perk waiting for you – luxury travel accommodations. Notice in Luke16:22 how Lazarus the beggar got to heaven: "And it came to pass, that the beggar died, and was <u>carried by the angels </u>into Abraham's bosom". Carried by angels! That has got to trump the most expensive first class seating aboard any earthly plane, train, or automobile. So dump the documents. They won't be needed either.

Okay, you've done your research, you've chosen God and His incredible gift of eternal life, and secured your transportation through Jesus' sacrifice on the cross. Do you feel your luggage getting even lighter? How about we lighten those suitcases to heaven a little bit more? You can probably throw away your foreign language dictionaries. Yes, there will be people from all over the world in heaven. In the book of Revelation, when John saw the "great multitude, which no man could number, of all nations, and kindreds, and people, and tongues" standing in front of God's throne in the eternal heaven, not only were they dressed in white and waving palm branches, they were shouting, "Salvation to our God which sitteth upon the throne, and unto the Lamb." (Revelation 7:9-10) Notice that, although there were people of many nationalities present, they all praised God with a singular voice. Also notice that the apostle John, who was witnessing this, could understand what was being said even though there were many languages being represented. He didn't need help translating what he heard. So you can ditch the foreign language dictionaries.

Let's look inside those heavenly suitcases one last time. You know what else isn't in there? Any items that you may have felt necessary for security purposes here on earth. Why? "For he that is dead is freed from sin." (Romans 6:7) That means sin in all its forms won't exist in heaven. Everything that threatened our safety and security will be a thing of the past. We won't have need of pepper spray, air horns, guns, or knives in heaven. This also means, humorously, that there won't be any long security-check point lines to wait in either. Just Jesus ready with a hearty "Welcome Home".

A sin-free heaven may sound somewhat simplistic, yet it goes much deeper than that in a couple of ways. First, the Greek word for sin in that verse is "hamartia" which translated means "to miss the mark, to miss or wander from the path of uprightness and honour, to do or go wrong, to wander from the law of God." Since we won't be wandering away from God or His laws when we are in heaven, we won't need any "roadmap to righteousness" so to speak. Secondly, since sin is not allowed in heaven, neither is sin's companions named guilt and shame.

Did you catch that? No longer will we be burdened with earthly guilt or shame. All too often in this present life we carry these around. Sometimes they are referred to as emotional baggage but a better description would be emotional backpacks. Suitcases are much easier to let go of whereas backpacks require a little more effort to be free of. They can be strapped to us and pull on our shoulders similar to how guilt and shame can pull on our hearts and minds. And even though when God forgives our sins and says He "will remember them no more" (Hebrews 10:17), we sometimes continue to beat ourselves up with our memories of past transgressions. God forgives and forgets; we on the other hand may be forgiven but we don't forget. Past transgressions cause emotional pain and come between us and pure peace. They tear at our minds and rob us of joy. Yet once we leave this life, we will drop every ounce of guilt and shame we have carried around needlessly. We will rise like an unfettered balloon, free of the sin that so easily entangles us here.

Now see inside those metaphorical suitcases? They are empty. In heaven you will have everything you need. Just as God has supplied all your needs here on earth (Philippians 4:19), He will do even more so in heaven. He is currently preparing a place for you in heaven. In heaven you'll be free of earthly cares and concerns. No more worries about unpaid bills, no mortgages to be met, no nervousness about what to wear or what to say. You'll also be free from the burden of all sin "which doth so easily beset us". It will be a spectacular eternal vacation indeed!

Home Sweet Home

We've finally arrived at our ultimate destination, the city of God, the eternal kingdom. After wandering around and exploring the temporary third heaven and enjoying all the perks that came with it, including reconnecting with family and friends, it is finally time to check out your new permanent accommodations. Christ has returned and brought with Him "new heavens and a new earth". Our new world is sinless, painless, and endless. On top of that the city of God has come down from heaven and is now a beautiful addition to the landscape. Can you see it? If it is still a little blurry let's see what the Bible tells us about our amazing new home to get a better mental picture.

First, it is HUGE! It has to be in order to accommodate so many "saints", those of us to whom the Bible refers as "holy and separate". Just exactly how big? According to Revelation 21:16, the city John saw was a perfect cube with the length, width, and height all being equal, each side being 12,000 furlongs. Since we don't currently use furlongs as a standard unit of measure, let's convert those measurements into something we are more familiar with. Are you sitting down? Twelve thousand furlongs is equal to 1,500 miles! That means that the city of God encompasses 2.25 MILLION square miles! Is that hard to wrap your mind around? If so, then these comparisons might help. The contiguous United States, what is sometimes referred to as "the lower 48", totals approximately 3.1 million square miles. Australia's total land area is about 2.97 million square miles. So if you took a clay model of either one of those examples, cut off the "appendages" or those portions of land that jutted out from the core area, then squared up what was left you're left with an approximation of one aspect of the city of God. See...huge!

If all of that isn't mind-boggling, let's add one further dimension to our mental picture of the "new Jerusalem". The city of God is as tall as it is wide. Did you catch that? It is 1,500 miles high! That translates to 3.375 BILLION cubic miles! Therefore when Jesus said, "In my Father's house are many mansions," he wasn't kidding. And if every citizen of heaven was given a quarter of a cubic mile, which is large enough for each mansion to have its own sizable park, then the city of God would be able to house 13.5 billion saints. That is, if every saint lived alone in their own expansive heavenly mansion. Granted, we all enjoy some solitude from time to time, but for eternity? Highly doubtful. That sounds more like how C.S. Lewis described hell in his book *The Great Divorce*. Dreadful thought. Let's move on to more pleasant thoughts and check out other details pertaining to that great city of God.

As you approach the New Jerusalem, more details will come into view. You will see the magnificent crystal walls with gates made of gigantic pearls and angels attending each gate. Passing through one of the gates you will see the main street made of purest gold and shining like glass leading to God's throne. The apostle John continues the description – "And I saw a river of water of life, clear as glass, coming out of the high seat of God and of the Lamb, in the middle of its street. And on this side of the river and on that was the tree of life, having twelve sorts of fruits, giving its fruit every month; and the leaves of the tree give life to the nations." (Revelation 22:1-2)

Now, would you like to peek inside the virtual windows of your own heavenly mansion that awaits you? To do so, simply close your eyes and picture what your dream home would look like on this earth. Think about all the unique touches you would add that suit your individual personality. Why would your eternal abode be different from everyone else's? Because God created you as a unique individual with particular likes and preferences. He created you with your own talents and abilities. As Psalm 139:14 says, you were "fearfully and wonderfully made". Therefore why wouldn't your heavenly home be as delightfully unique as you are? God is the Master Craftsman who knows you better than you know yourself. He is designing and furnishing your forever home to blend seamlessly with your own style. And don't expect the other houses in your neighborhood to be "cookie cutter" houses either. Remember, the other saints in heaven will come from "every kindred, and tongue, and people, and nation." The variety among the New Jerusalem neighborhoods will be amazingly beautiful.

Even though each of us has our own tastes and preferences in regards to housing styles and designs there will be a few features that every heavenly mansion will have in common. Since there will be feasting in heaven (more about that in the next chapter) there will probably be an appropriately sized kitchen. Then, because we'll be feasting with family and friends, there will be a sizable dining room in each home. On top of that each mansion will need to have plenty of space for socializing, so living rooms, rec rooms, game rooms and family rooms will be needed. We may also want rooms for resting in after going on "walk-abouts" or after joining a huge heavenly sing-a-long praising God, so plan on there being at least a few bedrooms (probably more appropriately called lounging rooms) included in the mansion blueprint for you and all your houseguests. Added to all these spaces there may even be a music room for groups of guests that want to have their own personal praise practices and a library for all the books on your favorite topics. Then, of course, there will be plenty of plush comfy seating throughout for all of your pious powwows and friendly fiestas.

Now, guess what you WON'T find in your eternal abode? As mentioned in previous chapters we'll have a limited wardrobe (a very good thing), so there won't be any walk-in closets or compact laundry rooms in your saintly home. There also probably won't be heating and air conditioning systems in our houses, since extreme temperatures cause pain and heaven will be pain-free. Next, the necessity of doors is questionable due to the fact that our glorified bodies, like Christ's, will be able to navigate into and out of places unencumbered. However, if you choose to have decorative doors throughout your mansion then don't plan on having locking doorknobs. Why will we need them? Take one final glimpse around your mansion and see if you can figure out what common earthly object is also missing from the many rooms. Here's a hint – if there will be no sickness in heaven that also includes colds and allergies. Yep, you guessed it. There won't be any boxes of tissues placed strategically throughout your heavenly house either.

Now that you've taken a quick peak inside your future home how about checking out other details pertaining to what lies outside those pearly gates. After all, when God allowed John to see the New Heaven and the New Earth, and said, "Behold, I make all things new" there were a LOT of new things and places for us to go, see, and do. Although John didn't get to see everything possible while he was there, we have clues as to what it will be like. In fact, many Bible scholars agree that in order to get a good mental picture of what the new Earth will look like, we simply have to go for a walk out in nature away from a city. You see, this earth we know now is simply a shadow of what God had already created in heaven prior to Him creating this earth. Have your doubts? In the book of Exodus, we are told that God called Moses to meet Him on Mount Sinai so that He could have a holy "show and tell" meeting with him. It was there that God told Moses to go down and build a temple among His chosen people camping at the base of the mountain that would be dedicated to holy worship and communion with God. He then showed Moses what it was to look like. One particular verse clearly indicates that the earthly temple was modeled after the heavenly one that God previewed to Moses. In the last verse of the twenty-fifth chapter, God told Moses, "And see that you make them from the design which you saw on the mountain." The earthly temple was modeled after the heavenly one.

There are several more indicators that point toward other things on this earth being modeled after what already existed in heaven. To begin with, the father-son relationship existed in heaven before it was created here on earth. There was also a tree of life in heaven prior to there being one in the earthly paradise we are told about in Genesis. That tree of life still exists in the city of God, the heavenly city that will be brought down to this earth after this fallen earth has been renewed. Finally, in Revelation 21 we are told that the first heaven and first earth will pass away when the new heaven and earth are ushered in. The Greek word for first is "protos" which implies a strong connection between first and second. This is similar to comparing a father and son. They are two distinctly different individuals who share many of the same characteristics. In short, many Bible scholars believe that the new heaven and new earth is modeled after what paradise was like before sin entered the world. There will be many similarities between old and new, just in a glorified state. It will be perfect, peaceful, and oh so pleasant.

With all this in mind, how about we go on a virtual "walkabout" of what is referred to in the book of Hebrews as a heavenly homeland. There are many references to what our eternal home will look like in the book of Isaiah. Here are just a few fabulous insights into what awaits us:

> Isaiah 11:6-7 And the wolf shall dwell with the lamb, and the leopard shall lie down with the kid; and the calf and the young lion and the fatling together; and a little child shall lead them. And the cow and the bear shall feed; their young ones shall lie down together; and the lion shall eat straw like the ox.
>
> Isaiah 41:18-20 I will make rivers flow on barren heights, and springs within the valleys. I will turn the desert into pools of water, and the parched ground into springs. I will put in the desert the cedar and the acacia, the myrtle and the olive. I will set pines in the wasteland, the fir and the cypress together, so that people may see and know, may consider and understand, that the hand of the LORD has done this, that the Holy One of Israel has created it.
>
> Isaiah 55:12-13 For ye shall go out with joy, and be led forth with peace: the mountains and the hills shall break forth before you into singing; and all the trees of the fields shall clap their hands. Instead of the thorn shall come up the fir-tree; and instead of the brier shall come up the myrtle-tree: and it shall be to Jehovah for a name, for an everlasting sign that shall not be cut off.
>
> Isaiah 65:21-25 And they shall build houses, and inhabit them; and they shall plant

vineyards, and eat the fruit of them. They shall not build, and another inhabit; they shall not plant, and another eat: for as the days of a tree shall be the days of my people, and my chosen shall long enjoy the work of their hands. They shall not labor in vain, nor bring forth for calamity; for they are the seed of the blessed of Jehovah, and their offspring with them. And it shall come to pass that, before they call, I will answer; and while they are yet speaking, I will hear. The wolf and the lamb will feed together, and the lion will eat straw like the ox, but dust will be the serpent's food. They will neither harm nor destroy on all my holy mountain," says the LORD.

Did you catch all the details within those few verses? There will be rivers in the mountains (heights), streams in the valleys, and springs in the deserts. There will be forests consisting of many types of trees scattered throughout the new earth. We'll be able to plant gardens and savor the harvests. We won't even be bothered with pesky weeds and thorns. If we want a country retreat, then we can build one outside the city. On top of all that, animals will live peacefully with each other and with us. How awesome will that be? We can wander among the wildebeests, lounge amongst the lions, meander among the monkeys. Or how would you like to have a pet tiger or gorilla? But the wonders of heaven don't stop there.

Do you like to play in the snow or dance in the rain? Do you enjoy listening to rolling thunder in the distance or hearing the pitter-pat of spring showers on the window? Good news! It seems highly likely that you'll be able to do all of those in heaven. Why will we be able do this? For the same reason the mountains will sing and the trees will clap. Because we are told in the book of Romans that everything God makes will praise and glorify Him. That includes the weather. We are told in the thirty-seventh book of Job that God sends the lightning, snow, and rain wherever He chooses. The big difference between this current earth and the new earth to come is that our heavenly earth won't be under the curse of sin like our fallen earth is. What can be harmful to us here will only glorify God there. Animals that are fierce and threatening here will be docile and playful there...all to glorify God. Aspects of weather that could be deadly here will only be glories to behold there...all to glorify God. The thorns and weeds that cause irritation and pain here won't exist there...all to glorify God. These earthly frail bodies that are subject to extremes in temperature won't be affected by them in the eternal heaven...all to glorify God.

Does all of this sound too good to be true? "The things which are impossible with men are possible with God." (Luke 18:27) "For who hath known the mind of the Lord? or who hath been his counsellor?" (Romans 11:34) "For as the heavens are higher than the earth, so are my ways higher than your ways, and my thoughts than your thoughts." (Isaiah 55:9) In short, even the most creative, scientific, intelligent human mind doesn't compare with the omniscience of God. If He can create billions and billions of humans without any two being exactly alike, if He knows how many stars are in the sky and has given each of them a name (Psalm 147:4), if He created everything in the entire universe by himself without any help or guidance from mere mortals, isn't it just possible that our eternal home will be beyond our wildest imaginations? Now, doesn't that take our breath away...or at least makes us pause and wonder?

Let's Get Busy
(or So Much To Do And So Much Time To Do It In)

Just in case there is anyone reading this that may still harbor concerns that eternity may be boring or that the activities there will be tedious and repetitious, this last chapter is specifically for you. From all of the verses we've looked at, and even more, God has given us some delightful details about what spending eternity with Him will be like. Think of the following as the most incredible itinerary or "to do" list imaginable.

Top on the list of activities is praising our heavenly Father. We'll join with the multitudes on a regular basis to sing, dance, and play musical instruments before the throne of God. We won't have to worry about being in tune because we'll all have glorified voices to go along with our glorified bodies. Dancing won't be an issue either for the same reason. We'll be able to twirl, bow, and kneel with ease. And, of course, for those who are gifted with musical talent will be accompanying us as our hearts are rejoicing at the wonder and goodness of the King of heaven.

Next on the "to do" list will depend on the individual skills God has endowed us with. Writers will be writing, sculptors will be sculpting, gardeners will be gardening, cooks will be cooking, builders will be building, and teachers will be teaching. So does the idea of working in heaven surprise you? If so, then is it possible you have never had a job here on earth that you enjoyed so much that it was more like play than work? Remember, before sin entered the world, Adam and Eve went about taking care of paradise without pain and sweat. It was only after their rebellion that "toil and sweat" entered the picture. After God redeems this earth, those will be things of the past, so to speak. We'll use the talents God has equipped us with to glorify Him without the burden of frail vulnerable bodies and minds. Creativity will flow uninhibited, the ground will produce abundance in weed-free, pest-free fields, meals and banquets will be prepared for regular feasting by kitchen artisans, mansion remodeling and additions will be painlessly constructed with skillful hands, and learning about God's immeasurable wisdom and knowledge will be endless and enjoyable. Work won't be a curse but a blessing.

Heaven won't be all praise and work though. There will be plenty of mirth and merriment too. We'll be able to have divine fellowship with those we were familiar with on this temporary earth as well as with a myriad of new friends and heavenly family members that we have yet to meet. We will gather in groups for game time, embark on expeditions to heavenly expanses together, and take delight in the new flora and fauna God will have created all around us. There will be meadows filled with flowers to meander through, streams and rivers to skip rocks across, mountains and hills to effortlessly explore, and a seemingly endless amount of animals to mingle with. On top of all this, there will be oh so many new faces to get to know. We'll be able to have discussions without getting defensive and debates without rancor. We'll embrace our differences and celebrate our similarities. All of this will still have a singular focus…glorifying the Lord of our new heaven and earth.

One other activity on the list is actually not an activity at all. Among all the blissful busyness that will occupy our heavenly schedules will be times of inactivity or rest. This won't be because we are tired but to give us time for reflection and renewal. In the book of Genesis we're told that after God created the world, He rested. He stepped back to view His creation and was pleased. Our times of rest will be used likewise. We'll be able to reflect on God's abundant goodness provided through our busyness and will renew our praises to Him.

Are you yearning for your heavenly home yet? If so, that is completely understandable. Satan is the prince of this world (John 12:31, 14:30) and as such followers of Christ yearn to be with Him and thus be free from the misery sin's curse has corrupted this present world with. The following lyrics underscore the original beauty created by the Maker of this world and should serve as a reminder of an even more beautiful world to come.

> This is my Father's world,
> And to my listening ears
> All nature sings, and round me rings
> The music of the spheres.
> This is my Father's world:
> I rest me in the thought
> Of rocks and trees, of skies and seas;
> His hand the wonders wrought.
>
> This is my Father's world,
> The birds their carols raise,
> The morning light, the lily white,
> Declare their maker's praise.
> This is my Father's world,
> He shines in all that's fair;
> In the rustling grass I hear him pass;
> He speaks to me everywhere.
>
> This is my Father's world.
> O let me ne'er forget

> That though the wrong seems oft so strong,
> God is the ruler yet.
> This is my Father's world:
> why should my heart be sad?
> The Lord is King; let the heavens ring!
> God reigns; let the earth be glad!

While on this present earth, there is still so much beauty to be seen that points the way toward what the eternal earth will be like. Focus on the good and don't let temporary circumstances rob you of your peace. Your faithfulness on this earth will definitely be rewarded accordingly in heaven. (Matthew 25) It will be beyond anything we can imagine. (Ephesians 3:20) We have "an inheritance incorruptible, and undefiled, and that fadeth not away, reserved in heaven" for us. And Jesus, along with so many others including our loved ones, are waiting at the finish line to wrap their arms around us and say with voices filled with love, "Welcome Home!"

Heaven Inspired Quotes

Perhaps they are not stars in the sky but rather openings where our loved ones shine down to let us know they are happy. -- Author Unknown

You will understand, of course, that Jesus is not going to wait until everyone is ready. He is coming and there will be a time when everyone will bow down before Him, both those who are ready and those who aren't. -- Corrie ten Boom

Eternity is a terrible thought. I mean, where's it going to end? -- Tom Stoppard

I can be at peace, knowing that what is eternal exceeds my understanding. -- Author Unknown

There are far better things ahead than any we leave behind. -- C.S. Lewis

You are free to choose but you are not free from the consequences of your choice. -- Zig Ziglar

My home is in Heaven. I'm just traveling through this world. -- Billy Graham

We're all just walking each other home. -- Ram Dass

The best remedy for those who are afraid, lonely or unhappy is to go outside, somewhere where they can be quiet, alone with the heavens, nature and God. Because only then does one feel that all is as it should be. -- Anne Frank

The fact that there's a highway to hell and only a stairway to heaven says a lot about anticipated traffic numbers. -- Anonymous

When I stand before God at the end of my life, I would hope that I would not have a single bit of talent left, and could say, 'I used everything you gave me.' — Erma Bombeck

If there are no dogs in Heaven, then when I die I want to go where they went. — Will Rogers

Heaven goes by favor. If it went by merit, you would stay out and your dog would go in. — Mark Twain

"Earth's crammed with heaven...But only he who sees, takes off his shoes." — Elizabeth Barrett Browning, *Aurora Leigh*

"I have come home at last! This is my real country! I belong here. This is the land I have been looking for all my life, though I never knew it till now...Come further up, come further in!" — C.S. Lewis, *The Last Battle*

Heaven is under our feet as well as over our heads. — Henry David Thoreau, *Walden*

I can safely say, on the authority of all that is revealed in the Word of God, that any man or woman on this earth who is bored and turned off by worship is not ready for heaven. — A.W. Tozer

We may be surprised at the people we find in heaven. God has a soft spot for sinners. His standards are quite low. — Desmond Tutu

If you die in an elevator, be sure to push the up button. — Sam Levenson

Death is nothing at all. It does not count. I have only slipped away into the next room. Why should I be out of mind because I am out of sight? I am but waiting for you, for an interval, somewhere very near, just round the corner. – Henry Scott Holland

Father, we thank You for all these relationships that teach us the important things in life are not what we own, but who we are, and who we love, and who loves us. We thank You for teaching us that Heaven has much to do with relationship, more than it has to do with location, as we will be the bride of Your son, to live eternally with Him, and with all our loved ones who have chosen to spend eternity with us. -- Jim Carmichael

Heaven "Want" List

For other publications by PenRose Editions visit:

PenRoseEditionsandPublishing.com